"The binding i ships: child to world; adolescent to friends; young woman to God, husband, children, and the past. Each poem explores these relationships with wit, a kind of melancholy gladness, and, finally, wisdom. You will find yourself in them and, yet, more than yourself. They are a pleasure—to the ear and to the soul."

~Daniel Taylor
Speaker and author of *Tell Me a Story* and
In Search of Sacred Places

"These poems provide eloquent testimony to the search for connections in life-connections that bind our personal identity to parents, grandparents, and children, and connections between faith and the suffering of loved ones. Penny Johnson explores the language of faith to discover connections that will surprise, console, and challenge you."

~Daniel E. Ritchie
Professor of English, Bethel University

"I suppose there are as many reasons to turn to poetry as there are readers of poetry, but surely most of us hope for a mix of seriousness and humor, intensity and groundedness that we can take with us back into our lives once we have finished the poem. Penny Johnson's poems offer just this kind of mix. Hers is a voice, it is easy to trust, and the poems themselves both challenge and inspire the reader. There are many poems I could point to that embody the qualities I'm describing here. One of my favorites is 'Jenny,' a poem that plays with our sense of identities and challenges us to see how permeable the boundary is between ourselves and the people around us we so often think of as strangers. From the first poem to the last, Penny Johnson treats her readers as friends rather than strangers: What a gift these poems are!"

~Jim Moore
Author of *Lightning at Dinner*

the last time

We Were Children

the last time

We Were Children

penny j. johnson

TATE PUBLISHING & Enterprises

Published by Tate Publishing & Enterprises, LLC
127 E. Trade Center Terrace | Mustang, Oklahoma 73064 USA
1.888.361.9473 | www.tatepublishing.com

Tate Publishing is committed to excellence in the publishing industry. The company reflects the philosophy established by the founders, based on Psalms 68:11,
"The Lord gave the word and great was the company of those who published it."

Book design copyright © 2007 by Tate Publishing, LLC. All rights reserved.
Cover design by Lindsay B. Behrens
Interior design by Elizabeth A. Mason

Published in the United States of America

ISBN: 978-1-6024733-0-x
07.04.03

To my grandfathers,
Clifford A. Olson and Gordon D. Nymann,
for their godly and Swedish perseverance
regardless of rank, education, or adversity

and

my grandmothers,
Sophie I. Olson and Anne M. Nymann,
for their gift of words through journals or
poetry and always through prayer.

Acknowledgements

Many thanks to the following:

Mr. Steve Althouse, my fifth grade teacher, who first encouraged me to write and read my work aloud, no matter how awful it was;

The English Department professors at Bethel University's College of Arts and Sciences in St. Paul from 1991–1994, who helped me develop my craft;

Jim Moore, my mentor through the Online Mentoring for Writers Split Rock Arts Program, who provided the right amount of encouragement and critique for each of these poems;

Peggy French, who included "Chicken a la King" in the Summer 2005 edition of *Shemom;*

The staff at Tate Publishing and Enterprises, who took a chance on me and this book;

Sarah Schoel, Diana Pederson, Trish Bjorklund, and Janel Kozlak, who read the manuscript graciously and objectively;

Charles Grafstrom, who proofread the final draft;

Countless extended family and friends who look forward to seeing my work published in something more than Christmas cards;

Paul and Pam Olson, my parents, who read, encouraged, and understood my need to write poetry even when doing math story problems;

Polly Merten and Peter Olson, my sister and brother, who read the manuscript as objectively as they were able;

Dave, my sweet husband, who loves me for who I am, makes up for what I am not, and keeps me laughing;

Nate, Jarrod, and Marcus, my three sons, who interrupt my writing moments with antics, challenges, and hugs, which somehow inspire more writing moments;

My current favorite poets—Tomas Tranströmer, Kjell Espmark, Anne Porter, Mary Oliver, Louise Glück, Annie Dillard, Lars Gustafsson, and Anna Swir—whose work inspired many of these poems;

And God, the First Author, who deserves all the glory and credit.

Contents

Author's Note

PART ONE

Chicken a la King 17

Jenny 18

One More Meal 20

Camp 21

After the Fair 22

The Field 23

Warmed Memories 24

PART TWO

Snow 27

Water Poems 31

Streets 36

PART THREE

After Cleaning 43

Write Me 44

Self-portrait 46

Asian Ladybird 47

Names 48

Offering 49

I promise praise and poetry 50

April and Silence   51

His Mother's Joy   52

On Watching a Church Choir One Sunday   53

Spring Breeze   54

Sestina   55

There must have been a world before   57

PART FOUR

First Day   61

The Pump   63

Make Me Believe in Christmas   65

Memorial   67

Last Words   68

Memory Care   70

Phone Call   71

Stranger   74

For Peter   75

Flo   76

After a Conversation with My Husband   77

On Raising Boys   78

Vespers   79

Holy War   80

Kyrie   81

On Staying Up All Night with a Sick Child   82

Matins   83

Adjusting the Darkness   84

Where is the island that changes ours lives?   87

Author's Note

I am often inspired by what I read. Scripture, novels, essays, and poems all bring me to a greater understanding of life and my place in it as a woman and a writer. There are fellow poets who directly influenced the poems in this book whether in titles, lines, or style. Endnotes document those bits of influence from others. The poem "Write Me" is perhaps the most influenced. It is a found poem in which all of the lines, including the title, are from poems by Swedish poet Kjell Espmark. Any changes I made were in punctuation, verb tense, and one noun ("man" to "woman"). In pulling lines from his poems, I created an original poem describing the struggles of a writer, specifically my own. I mention the influences of these poems for two reasons: I believe in giving credit where credit is due, and because I believe in supporting the work of fellow writers. If my poems inspire you, read the poets who have inspired me.

On that note, if there is a Scripture reference cited, look it up. No author has affected my work more than the One True Author. Because of the same two reasons, I give God credit, for it is due him, and support his work with mine because I believe what he has written. Read it! May it inspire you as well.

-P.J.J.

When I was a child, I talked like a child, I thought like a child, I reasoned like a child. When I became a [woman], I put childish ways behind me. Now we see but a poor reflection as in a mirror; then we shall see face to face. Now I know in part; then I shall know fully, even as I am fully known.

1 Corinthians 13:11–12, NIV (insertion mine).

PART ONE

CHICKEN A LA KING
for Nate

I make Chicken a la King
for the first time
and remember
sitting at a white speckled table
after a Saturday night bath
with pink curlers in my hair.

A memory
of a chicken mixture over toast?
I don't even like chicken.
What are pimientos anyway?

But after I serve my oldest son
after I ask a question my mother asked me—
"do you want it on the side or on top of?"—
after he tastes it and says
"I don't like it,"

I place the spoon in the bowl,
stirring up the memory
bright red as the pimientos.
It pops up warm,
soaking in deep like melted butter.

JENNY

Sometimes I think about it—

Walking my doll up 5th Street in Anoka
in her green and white stroller with the white wheels.

Even at age five, I walked around the block alone.
At the corner in front of the gas station

with the orange circle on a metal stick
that looked like a lollipop,

two heads—one with dark, curly hair,
one balanced on a white sweater collar—

looked in on each side of my vision
as if they were cartoons looking around a doorframe.

Is your name Jenny? White Collar asked.
No, I said.

They ran past the white picket fences
in a strange frenzy,

as if playing a game,
yet one that would make them smile that way.

I finished my walk home
and ate a peanut butter-jelly sandwich.

But when I think of those faceless heads,
the name *Jenny* instead of *Penny*,

that I finished my walk,

I wonder if Jenny made it home
to her peanut butter-jelly sandwich.

ONE MORE MEAL

I see a lighted kitchen,
five people around an heirloom table:
the one who asks the questions,
the one who talks too much,
the one who remains silent,
the one who gives an eye roll,
the one who listens over the sink and dirty dishes.

CAMP

I swat at bees that sting my finger.
Mom removes the stinger.
Dad sets fire to their hive.

My friend drowns my doll.
My pail's handle floats away
over broken shells on the lake bottom.

If I go alone, I will be homesick
for pink curlers, Chapel Hill,
and the bell ringing each morning.

AFTER THE FAIR

The first week in August,
the county fairgrounds near the river
teem with locals and visitors,
waiting in lines for the Ferris Wheel,
staggering off the Tilt-a-Whirl,
buying another beer or something
mixed with its batter,
throwing rings or shooting guns
for toys filled with sawdust,
shuffling feet on straw-covered floors,
and resting them under grand stand bleachers.

But, after the fair,
I have free admission
to ride old tractor trailers,
call horse races from the sound booth,
or gallop the track myself.
I attend the one-room school,
sell popcorn at abandoned booths with stone money,
run off ramps to become the next great attraction.

THE FIELD

I play in the prairie with children
over a century ago just beyond
their one-room school.

My feet sink into gophers' roofs
and burrs stick to my laces,
pricking through my socks.

I balance on a natural footbridge
over a brook hidden
in a grove of birch trees.

This field is across a highway
where cars hit my grandparents' dogs.
Here we find strays to love again.

I play in the prairie with children
over a century ago just beyond
their one-room school,

now just a foundation hole.

WARMED MEMORIES

On New Year's Eve,
Mom takes the family calendar from its nail;

our family of five flips through the months,
then Mom tears each page from the spiral

throws it into the flames.
We watch the paper curl and char.

Such a violent way
to end and begin a year?

Some memories, the hot ones,
I want turned to cinders.

But some pages spark their own fires,
warming my back on my coldest days.

PART TWO

SNOW[1]

The Hill

One year we discovered the best sledding hill
right in our back yard along the banks of the Rum River.
After Dad whacked away the wood weeds,
every kid in the neighborhood spent the day

> sliding,
> climbing,
> sliding,
> climbing

until our wrists were bright red under the snow
that became our coat cuffs.
We thought it was the perfect hill
until we used a toboggan,
and one of the girls crashed into a fallen tree at the bottom.
Even after her cast came off,
and Dad removed the tree,
the kids found other hills.
This only meant I didn't have to share mine anymore.

St. Louis Snowstorm

I knew I needed you
when less than three inches
closed schools in St. Louis,
and no one understood
there wasn't enough of you.

Halloween Blizzard, October 31, 1991

An act of God
stranded me
at my boyfriend's house
overnight?
But then, it was the devil's night
of tricks disguised as treats.
I tricked him back
by waking with the saints
on the couch.

My Birthday, 1999

My husband learned the lesson
that he should never
buy presents for himself
on my birthday,
especially a snowmobile,
because you stayed away
for three years
and didn't return
until he sold it.

May 1, 2004

I must admit
I think it's time
you stayed home
in the clouds.

Why do I love you?
Why do I need to live
where you fall
not just in inches, but in feet
so that my own sink
into your depths,
my boots becoming cups
for you to fill?

It's no more
than remembering
the thrill of sledding hills.

WATER POEMS[2]

1. Swimming Lessons

Groping,
Reaching out
For what I knew
Was there
Just inches
From my fingers,
Until
Feeling strong
Hands hoisting me
From one
Element
To another,
Coughing
Out what's breathed
When underneath
I held in
Every breath.

My next lesson:
To open
My eyes.

2. Reflecting on the Death of a Young Artist
for Josh
1 Peter 1:24–25

As I sing Brahms' *Requiem,* the second movement,
I imagine you standing on the bank of the St. Croix,
and I wonder if you were painting a picture in your head
as the August grass browned under the heat of the sun.

I imagine you standing on the bank of the St. Croix,
the river that washed your life away downstream,
as the August grass browned under the heat of the sun
before the canvas blackened completely.

The river that washed your life away downstream
sends an instant thought of you when I hear its name.
Before the canvas blackened completely,
did Christ give you the first eternal word?

Sends an instant thought of you. When I hear its name,
I see you, a talented artist, dying in a watery field.
Did Christ give you the first eternal word
as your art became immortalized?

I see you, a talented artist, dying in a watery field,
see your hair like brush bristles paint swirls in the sand—
your last artwork immortalized.
Clearly, you were capable of great things.

I see your hair like brush bristles paint swirls in the sand
as I sing Brahms' *Requiem,* the second movement.
You were capable of such great things,
and I wonder what picture you were painting in your head.

3. LILY PADS

Lily pads,
Green heart
Of the river, stand
Firm enough to float,
Allow boats through,
      Moving aside.
      This carpet is
Too weak for a child
To cross to an island,
Yet supports a frog
As he drinks from
A floral cup.

4. THE LAST TIME WE WERE CHILDREN
for Carla, Jeff, Polly, Peter, and Me

The last time we were children
we sat on the rocky edge of the Atlantic,

let its waves imbed salt
under our skin until we itched.

I wore my wedding ring that told me I was old
enough to live beyond the games we used to play,

but not too old to dare to itch
for the young days when I wasn't brave,

couldn't jump from fifty-foot cliffs, yet
on this edge could suddenly swim with jellyfish.

STREETS

1. SOMEWHERE IN CHAMPLIN, MN

I am a photograph
of a baby
sitting in an old armchair,
smiling,
at a thought
her brain under a soft spot
cannot recall.

2. MADISON STREET, ANOKA, MN

In our little red wagon,
Mommy pulls my sister and me to town;
on my green Schwinn,
I travel the four corners of my world;
on my backyard swing,
I try to touch tree branches with my toes—
here,
my only fear
is stepping
on sidewalk cracks.

3. Rum River Drive, Anoka, MN

I think
of the window in my room,
of pink,
of a river that flows
behind trees
in front of me,
of how a child never knows
that wanting to run away
will make her wish she'd stayed.

4. Bear Branch Court, Chesterfield, MO

At the heart
of a round, cement cul-de-sac
we cry,
sighing "goodbye,"
dying to make the U-turn home.

5. Foothill Trail, Vadnais Heights, MN

I am still there,
standing at the edge
of the driveway
at my last childhood home,

watching their white Silhouette
drive to the end of our street
on the day my parents left home.

6. Windwood Drive, Dublin, OH

It looks like my room;
with the maple desk and dresser,
the dolls in pink on the bed,
the boxes in the hutch full of letters,
the books on the shelf I once read;
but it isn't
because this room needs dreams,
and I cannot give it mine.

7. Great View Avenue, Brooklyn Center, MN

I carry my over-packed suitcase,
stuffed with journals—
half-filled or blank—
poetry on loose-leaf paper,
and every book I own,
and even though it contains
all I need to survive
even after I arrive
I sit on it,
straining the locks closed.

8. Bethel Drive, Arden Hills, MN

We live like sisters
cramming our brains with facts
for tests we ought to pass
to earn our degrees
in "Friendships That Last."

9. Carmel Court, Shoreview, MN

My cart overflowing
with ant and shrew traps,
a clothesline, a laundry tub,
ceiling plaster, a large bucket,
and pregnancy tests,
I search the aisles
wondering all the while
if I can afford a sense of humor.

10. Sunnyside Terrace, New Brighton, MN

Listening to the quiet
spring breeze through leaves,
a mourning dove's coo,
I stroke my swelling belly,
smiling a silent sigh,
believing in this street's sunny side.

11. 155ᵀᴴ Avenue NW, Andover, MN

It's too far,
some say,
to follow the North Star
to walk toward the setting sun.

12. The Road Ahead

PART THREE

AFTER CLEANING

Socks on vacuumed carpet—
soft, padding on fluffed fibers—
a hint of pine—fresh breath for the room.

My pen moving across blank pages,
padding on tight parchment,
breathing in perfumed ink, exhaling words like clover blooms.

WRITE ME[3]

A FOUND POEM BASED ON THE POETRY OF KJELL ESPMARK.

When a language dies,[4]
the frozen words on the page repelling their meaning,[5]
the rain on fossil lips making language obsolete,[6]
the smile where the poem has vanished,[7]

what do we mean by 'recognize,'[8]
words like 'chronology' and 'explanation'?[9]
There are no words.[10]
Thought is captive in the engraved pattern.[11]
I spell my way through the foreign text.[12]
Half the letter is written.[13]
Halfway through, the letter was over.[14]

You who polish words while waiting for the dawn,[15]
see how it fares with a woman
from whom God has turned His face?[16]
Without you language would turn its back on us.[17]
The message altered into something neither of us intended;[18]
our faces dare to leave us.[19]

"It's only me who knows," cries the paperboy.[20]
"Do you know it's you misunderstanding?[21]
Just come a little closer."[22]

He knows.[23]
He is sitting inside the answer.[24]

The picture in the cave has been lifted into the paper.[25]
The scent of lilac is suddenly a phrase.[26]
Among the merciless lines of the engraving,[27]
the word is grace.[28]

SELF-PORTRAIT

Peeling, parchment-like bark,
lined by the bleed-through
of my black-inked soul.

ASIAN LADYBIRD

As I get ready one morning,
I see you walk across the mirror,

your reflection, your dark underside
is all you see, just as I cannot see

my own back without another
mirror, reflection of a reflection.

Have you never seen who
you really are, your red side

with distinctive spots?
Your friends must know you by them.

If you split your wings to fly
do you see them then?

Stunned suddenly, do you tuck them
quick behind your head

so certain they don't belong to you,
that such beauty could never be yours?

NAMES

My real name is Swedish *flicka*
       collecting plates with blue and yellow flowers.
Yesterday my name was laundry maid
       and bread maker.
Today my name will be weaver
       of threaded words.
Secretly my name is Wild Daisy
       and Forget-Me-Not.
My name was once of simple
       coppery quality necessary for making change.

OFFERING

I gave you my life,
when I was five,
sitting on the stairs,
looking up at the ceiling,
and praying you into my heart.

I give myself to you
this moment,
sitting in the palm of your hand,
looking toward your purpose,
until I have nothing left to give.

I PROMISE PRAISE AND POETRY

until

    I forget how to write words

my

    identity shadowed by

fire

    becoming a reverted element as passion

goes

    beyond sense drives instinct

out[29]

    before the last escape.

APRIL AND SILENCE [30]

The leaves of perennials
So crushed and wilted,
I forget what they are called.

As on those three days, the sun un-risen
Until the sudden exhale
Strong enough to roll away a stone;

That moment when a single bud
Rose from that leafy heap,
And, among all the others, called my name.

HIS MOTHER'S JOY

Did she realize in her wonderment,
as she played with her child's feet still wet just after birth,
held his tiny wrist and stroked the cushy center of his palm,
watched his round belly rise and fall,
laughed as she tickled his side,
believed that in him through his birth her joy was complete,
that one day
she would touch her child's feet still wet just after death,
hold his wounded wrist and stroke the cushy center of his palm,
watch his sunken belly still,
weep as she rubbed his pierced side,
believe that in him through his death her joy would be complete?

ON WATCHING A CHURCH
CHOIR ONE SUNDAY

Notes glide from beneath bow on strings,
trombone slide ties the melody, trumpet bursts declare,
and well-known words slip from tongue tips,
yet no smiles, no eyes alight
only glares on glasses, vacant stares—
Where? Where! Where is joy on weary masks
creased with wrinkling cares
with mouths in motion yet no emotion,
and gazes down instead of

up. See! See with eyes closed to darkness, to despair.
Let lyrics lick wounds and repair the weeping soul.
Can you hear as I hear, see me with my love in the balcony,
his murmuring voice singing music he learned alone
while I knelt for years in prayer?

SPRING BREEZE

I step outside
See two bumblebees on rhododendrons
Long to see them on lilac trees
Their June scent on the wind
That blows and blows my hair, saturates it.
Only God can breathe it,
Its sweetness even before rain.

SESTINA

John 15:1–17

Moses met the Lord face to face on a mountain
named Sinai while the people in the valley
worshiped a golden image, forgetting to abide
in the one who spoke to Moses, who reflected his light
in the face of a mere man, who dwelled in a cloud without rain,
who fed them in the desert, and who heard each slaves' call.

Sometimes I have to travel to hear his call
the way I heard it in Wyoming, climbing a mountain
named Laramie, the brim of my sailor hat filling with rain,
racing myself to the top, seeing a double rainbow over the valley,
climbing over slick rocks standing on end, the evening light
coming through the cave's cleft. This my first lesson in "abide."

Christ talked to his disciples about how to abide
in him by following his commands, calling
on him for all things, in the waning light
after Passover, as they walked in the vineyard of the Mount

of Olives, before Jesus prayed, before walking the Kidron Valley,
that place of black betrayal, that is dead dry without rain.

I sat on the couch, my legs refusing to move, trying to refrain
from self-pity when I heard clearly the word "Abide."
I didn't understand at first. Maybe I was too deep in the valley
of regret and confusion. But, I knew his voice, his call
to leave what I thought was best, meet him on the mountain
of his grace, where we are friends, and simply enjoy his light.

After his death, after his resurrection, after 40 days the Light
of the World ascended in a cloud without rain
from the place where he last prayed, the olive mountain,
to heaven where he forever abides
at the right hand of God. And he says those who hear his call
will meet him in the sky and escape the darkest of valleys.

3,015 days; 2,075 days; the lengths of my longest valleys
and counting. Somehow the dark days enlighten.
Why true? But it is. When I recall
all the times little glimmers mean more than rain's
lightning that splits and chars, I hear "Abide"
and know not far off there waits another mountain.

THERE MUST HAVE BEEN
A WORLD BEFORE[31]

the static sigh of an alarm
clock, the cock's crow replaced by electric shock,

the shush of children's feet on carpet
on tip-toe, face close to touch my nose;

my love faking sleep
breath deep, brief caress before I dress;

the day remains unknown
no human plan, no firm command

like the moment before God
spoke on the first morning, broke the world awake.

PART FOUR

FIRST DAY

For my parents

On the first day of school in 1962,
The boy sat behind the new girl in class,
Her brown bob hanging above her straight back,
Her hands clasped, probably hoping it wouldn't happen again.
But it did—
        "If I didn't call your name, please stand up."
He heard her exasperated sigh, saw her shoulders slump,
As she stood and for the sixth time that day,
Gave her first name—one uniquely beautiful—
And her last name—the same as the new superintendent,
Her well-organized father, who somehow forgot to register her.
The boy knew she resented being forced to make herself known,
And he knew he would stop at nothing to know her better.

The girl wondered if the boy would ever stop bothering her,
Complained about him to her mother,
Who only smiled and giggled at her frustration.
She suffered through his chatting before classes began,
How he contentedly talked to the back of her head,

Didn't seem put off by another boy's name on her notebook.
For four years, she refused to like him, until
After their first kiss—in a play on a stage—
He asked her outright if she loved him,
And with the same exasperated sigh
She murmured yes, knowing he knew
She could no longer pretend otherwise.

THE PUMP
for Dad

The water you pumped in 30-below weather
cannot wash the orange stain from your palms,
the rust that seeps into your veins.

As you bumped ice chips from the pump spout,
your knuckles under handmade wool mittens
creaked along with the handle,
a sound that sticks in your head like a bad song
reminding you of an unfinished cottage
with exposed electrical wires and peeling paint;
the food—boxed potatoes, corn bread, rice with raisins,
and oatmeal so thick your mother served it on a plate;
your mother's sulking and your father's silence;
your father's heart attack and early death.

You pumped that handle harder,
never stopping,
as you paid your way through college,
married your high school sweetheart,
made it to the NFL,

had three children,
became a computer-industry pioneer,
made your first million,
because you stored that pump in your garage,
then placed it in the garden
like a tombstone over buried memories,
those remnants of ice-cold pain
burning your fingers frostbite red.

MAKE ME BELIEVE
IN CHRISTMAS
for Clifford A. Olson (1909–1978)
and
for Nate and all children who seek the truth

⁂

"Is there such a thing as Santa?"
my child asked on his eighth Christmas,
with the same indignant scowl
he gave when he received
a present wrapped in the same paper
I used to wrap his teacher's gift.
Not knowing how to answer for a legend
I'd never really told,
but had never denied,
or ever believed myself
since discovering my own gifts
on shelves, unwrapped, at age four,
I told him a story . . .

A little boy, who was not quite old enough to know
he was poor because he still survived on dreams,
went to see Santa at the mall. Sitting on the edge of

the bearded man's knee, he shared his secret wishes not even his father knew. But, wanting to know more about the man inside the red coat, he left his mother, pushed apart a curtain, and entered a forbidden place where a clean-shaven man in a T-shirt and Santa's pants yelled, "Get out!"

The startled boy backed away into the white-cuffed, red-velvet arms of his Santa, who looked at him with tender blue eyes like his own, picked him up with carpenter-worked hands like his father's, and carried him to his mother, who gave Santa a kiss on the cheek before they left for home.

"The little boy was my father,
and the Santa was his father,"
I said with a telling smile.
And in that moment
my child believed in Christmas
without the make-believe.

MEMORIAL

For Sophie Inga Hunt Clark Olson (1910–1999)

A rose, slightly bent,
fragile as last breaths.

I stifle an exhale
and slink away,

afraid to touch it
to watch it fade:

This reminder of my inability to see
my grandmother before she died.

LAST WORDS
for Gordon D. Nymann (1922–2002)

As my grandfather was wheeled into an ambulance
On his last day on earth,
This son of Sweden
This lieutenant of WWII and Korea
This husband of nearly 58 years
This father of two daughters
This grandfather of five
This scholar with three degrees
This superintendent of schools
This man I could count on to drive me to the airport
This man who could talk about anything with anyone
This, the most profound man I've ever known

Said
Because he always valued a dollar
        And knew, for even a day,
        the nursing home would cost him
Because he knew he had lost his cancer battle
        And couldn't care for the wife he loved
        until she forgot his name
Because he loved God,
        Yet couldn't understand why he simply
        couldn't die in his sleep
His last words:
"What a bummer!"

MEMORY CARE
For AMGN

"I wanted to stay as I was,"
I imagine her saying,
(if she were one to complain)
as she flips through old photographs

of beaches at high tide before sunscreen
when skin browned naturally and ignored the burn,

of sitting on her honey's lap before the war and after aging battles,
looking past the wrinkles,

on their silver anniversary, standing with her daughters, pointing,
joking with her man behind the camera,

of posing on piano benches poised to play anything from Chopin
to her favorite hymns,

of pouring cranberry juice in teacups for grandchildren,
watching them eat her paper-thin sugar cookies,

of watching *Matlock* reruns, knitting for no one
but the next person she met.

PHONE CALL

The phone ringing on Sunday morning is never a good sign.

I had just thought last night that I don't call you enough.
And I'm right.

Somehow I beat the ambulance to the church
and avoid a ticket.

Everyone is staring at the flashing lights,
wondering what's happening,

And I know they are for you, for me.
I grab your clammy hand and see you know me.

Behind an oxygen mask, you answer
"How are you feeling?" with "Stupid."

I feel stupid, too, as the paramedic asks
About medications, doctors' names, clinics.

I forget to fasten my seatbelt
As I follow the ambulance.

I enter the ER and am amazed
You have priority.

And so we sit, and wait,
For tests, listening to the heart monitor beep.

You keep telling me that I'm so good to put up with you.
I tell you to rest, and you refuse, your eyelids closing anyway.

I watch you, breathing gap-mouthed, glad for the sound,
Wondering how I came to be here.

I would rather be eating pancakes at your house
And staying overnight, sleeping on fresh linens.

I made pancakes yesterday for the boys the way you did,
Barely browned and small with the same syrup.

You pop awake and gasp, grabbing my hand,
"Oh, I'm so glad to see you!"

I ask if you know where you are
And you don't,

So I tell the story of how we got here,
The one you will never remember, will deny later.

You will pull out your IV and heart monitor cords,
Get out of bed, try to walk through three nurses.

You will be very sweet about it,
Smiling as you always do.

STRANGER
for Polly

She doesn't know us today—
She asks me to introduce you.
She gives my name, my identity,
To the aide who brings her in.

But, then,

Who is this woman who enters,
Her hair all wrong?
Everything is where it ought to be—
>the King James Bible on the tea cart,
>the country hymnal above the keyboard,
>penciled notes in knitting books.

The black cricket still stops the door, but it closes anyway
Behind this woman
Who we no longer recognize as our Grandma
Whose treasures—
And we two among them—
Fill this room.

FOR PETER

I never knew you
hated being known

for great intelligence,
those fine fingers

moving over keys,
black and white,

lyric calm
over suppressed emotions,

your identity defined by what your life contains
rather than being known by name.

FLO

She's back for another visit.
For a whole week I anticipate her,
For a whole week I put up with her,
For a whole week I smile that's she gone.

I blame her for many things—
a burst of temper, a forgotten watch,
a dropped glove or worse a glass,
the feeling that everything is too close

and I want nothing to do with touch.

Maybe she's why I never had a daughter
because I don't want to explain
why she has to come, why she's necessary
to make you who you are.

I find peace in throwing part of her away,
in one less visit to anticipate,
in one more to prepare and give her room
to teach me how I should respond.

AFTER A CONVERSATION
WITH MY HUSBAND

You do not understand
my lines of poetry any more
than I understand
your lines of computer code.

You do not understand
my metaphorical speech,
explaining life by connecting
image to image.

I do not understand
your cyberspace games
without endings, no winners,
connecting with unknown friends.

How is it then
we can know
what each is thinking
and sometimes even speak in unison?

ON RAISING BOYS

Each day I've been a mother of boys, I realize
I know nothing
except what can be learned
from the mistakes I made the day before.

VESPERS[32]

I think about
a child left to lie on his back for two and a half years
by his parents
until the bones above his surgically-repaired heart
healed into a peak,
the only thing saving him from their pornography ring
an extra chromosome, which rewarded him with neglect.

I, then, regret
brushing my son's hand away
instead of letting him fidget with my hair
when all he wanted was tangible comfort
while I clung to resentment about his less than perfect day
at school . . .

that he is less than perfect.

What's the difference?

Is it enough that I held my child's hands
and with him prayed tomorrow would be better?

HOLY WAR

What does it mean when towers fall,
steel planes piercing pillars' sides,
bodies destined to be unidentified;

On hands and knees, we claw and scrape;
our safety lost in soot,
our hope disintegrated dust?

In the rubble, we mumble;
our prayers spoken momentarily in a unified voice
as pleading psalms of rescue, redemption, and release.

KYRIE[33]

My life discovered beauty through studying its scars:
in the creases of my disease-filled eyelids,
on the edge of my laugh lines—
the removal of bone and tissue to bring healing.

Like our son smiling at jokes—
both funny and cruel—misunderstood,
who somehow failed to feel a broken arm after carrying—
maybe riding—a rocking horse down a flight of sixteen stairs.

ON STAYING UP ALL NIGHT
WITH A SICK CHILD

for Marcus

Only a mother
listens at doorframes
for deep sleep breathing
but moves closer at the rasps,
gets the father for a second opinion
before deciding to sleep with the child
in a recliner next to a table with tissues, a book,
her glasses in case she needs to see as well as hear
the breathing blowing on her cheek all night, stirring
her away from sleep she's willing to give up when her baby
in his croaky voice whispers, "Mommy? I love you," before
he sleeps.

MATINS[34]

Why are moments like this still morning so easily missed:
to see the day not as dark, ignoring the prelude to light
when all is silent and I might actually hear the voice of God?

ADJUSTING THE DARKNESS
Inspired by Jarrod and 2 Corinthians 4:6–9, 15–18

I. RESTLESS NIGHTS

I realize in moments, when God's voice seems silent
when undefined fear keeps me behind a locked door
when I'm trapped in twisted sheets
when my uncertain thoughts toss and turn,
throughout days that seem like eternal nights,
I must imagine familiar faces of survival framed in the hall,
hear floor creaks and water running through pipes,
find comfort in the light under the door,
for *sometimes my life opened its eyes in the dark.*[35]

II. NIGHTMARES AND DAYDREAMS

I make beds
while I wait for the word
"autism"
to enter my daily routine.

My son is on display
in the grocery store.
I would attempt to explain
his flailing arms,

his heels kicking my shins,
his fixation on a blue light saber
for the skeptical, fearful, judging eyes
gawking at him in wild surprise.
These onlookers
standing at a distance,
scoffing and walking away,
or worse
speaking without understanding
see only what they are.
So I pretend the store is empty.

I forget about Job's loss of loved ones and land
when a clear word from my child
reminds me
that darkness is not what I see.

III. Dawn

Sometimes my life opened its eyes in the dark[36]
with my son's fierce tapping on my shoulder,
urging me toward uncovering
before embarking
on the expedition of discovery
of what I am not sure.
He invites me because I am his mother.
I place my feet on solid ground,
taking pleasure in the stretching of unused limbs.

WHERE IS THE ISLAND THAT CHANGES OUR LIVES?[37]

On Crane Lake, on a sand beach—
Not like the rock shore we crashed into
Or the soft one that sucked off my shoes—

The carved bench near the fire pit
Says others claimed this spot
But for this week it is ours.

My youngest son goes with me and our hound dog
Down the paths. We go just so far, head back,
The next time go a bit farther.

I drape an arm over my second son
As we ride behind the boat
On a float the size of a couch.

On a rock peninsula, my oldest son emerges
From his own alone time. We talk,
I forget about what, yet I know it is significant.

Every morning, we wake to the call of loons,
My husband and I, remembering what started—
Different topographies on the same island.

Before we leave,
We add our names to the bench,
Hoping we'll be back to carve in more years.

Endnotes

1. Style inspired by Mary Oliver, "Rain," *New and Selected Poems,* (Boston: Beacon Press, 1992), p. 3–7.

2. Ibid.

3. Robin Fulton, trans., *Five Swedish Poets,* "The Other Life," by Kjell Espmark, (Norwich: Norvik Press, 1997), p. 36.

4. Fulton/Espmark, "When a language dies . . . ," p. 25.

5. Fulton/Espmark "Letter Writing 2," p. 41.

6. Fulton/Espmark "Caribbean Quartet 2," p. 45.

7. Fulton/Espmark "Letter Writing 2," p. 40.

8. Fulton/Espmark "Prague Quartet 1," p. 18.

9. Fulton/Espmark "The Other Life," p. 35.

10. Fulton/Espmark "Caribbean Quartet 2," p. 45.

11. Fulton/Espmark "Caribbean Quartet 1," p. 44.

12. Fulton/Espmark "Prague Quartet 3," p. 20.

13. Fulton/Espmark "Letter Writing 1," p. 40.

14. Fulton/Espmark "Letter Writing 2," p. 41.

15. Fulton/Espmark "Caribbean Quartet 3," p. 46.

16. Fulton/Espmark "Family Memory," p. 42.

17. Fulton/Espmark "Caribbean Quartet 3," p. 46.

18. Fulton/Espmark "Letter Writing 3," p. 41.

19. Ibid.

20. Fulton/Espmark "Caribbean Quartet 1," p. 44.

21. Fulton/Espmark "Four Greek Voices from under the Ground 3," p. 32.

22. Fulton/Espmark, "Four Greek Voices from under the Ground 4," p. 33.

23. Fulton/Espmark, "Life for Sale," p. 38.

24. Fulton/Espmark, "Jotted on History's Margin 7," p. 29.

25. Fulton/Espmark, "Archetype," p. 42.

26. Fulton/Espmark, "Prague Quartet 1," p.18.

27. Fulton/Espmark, "Caribbean Quartet 1," p. 45.

28. Fulton/Espmark, "The Other Life," p. 36.

29. Anne Porter, "A Song of Fear and Fire," *Living Things: Collected Poems,* (Hanover: Zoland Books, 2006), p. 27.

30. See similar title in Tomas Tranströmer, "April and Silence," trans. Robert Bly, *The Half-Finished Heaven: The Best Poems of Tomas Tranströmer,* (St Paul: Graywolf Press, 2001), p. 94.

31. Lars Gustafsson, "The Stillness of the World Before Bach," *The Stillness of the World Before Bach:*

New Selected Poems, ed. Christopher Middleton (New York: New Directions Books, 1988), p. 95.

32. See similar titles in Louise Glück, *The Wild Iris* (Hopewell: The Ecco Press, 1992).

33. See similar title in Tomas Tranströmer, "Kyrie", *Selected Poems* 1954–1986, ed. Robert Hass, (New York: The Ecco Press, 1987), p. 36.

34. See similar titles in Louise Glück, *The Wild Iris* (Hopewell: The Ecco Press, 1992).

35. Tranströmer, p. 36.

36. Ibid.

37. Gustafsson, "Declaration of Love to a Sephardic Lady," p. 44.